FLORIATED ORNAMENT

A Series of Thirty-one Designs.

BY

AUGUSTUS WELBY PUGIN,
Architect.

" Consider the lilies of the field, how they grow ; they toil not, neither do they spin : and yet I say unto
you, That even Solomon in all his glory was not arrayed like one of these."

First published by
HENRY G. BOHN, YORK STREET, COVENT GARDEN, LONDON
MDCCCXLIX

Reprinted by
RICHARD DENNIS, SHEPTON BEAUCHAMP, SOMERSET
MCMXCIV

ISBN 0 903685 36 1

PREFACE

During his short but remarkably creative life, the architect A.W.N. Pugin (1812–1852) placed design and architecture on a new footing influencing the course of British and European architecture for the rest of the century. He wrote, illustrated and designed several books, but *Floriated Ornament* is without doubt the most beautiful. It was long in the making for he referred to it in 1845 whilst campaigning to improve the teaching of design in this country. This is the clue to his purpose, which was to reform the application of natural forms to mass-produced objects.

By the late 1840s plant ornament ran riot, bunches of cabbage roses appeared to be strewn on carpets and honeysuckle to grow up curtains and wallpaper. Designers and manufacturers expended great efforts to make these plants look as three dimensional and realistic as possible. If you read Pugin's own clearly written Introduction you will see he argues that in the middle ages flat pattern was so successful because the plants were flattened and arranged in abstract rather than naturalistic ways.

Pugin himself applied these principles to stencilling the interiors of his buildings, also to ceramics, wallpapers, carpets, curtains, furniture, stained glass and tiles. Examples of these Pugin objects were seen by millions at the 1851 Exhibition and were to furnish many homes over the next fifty years. Indeed Minton kept one of Pugin's tableware designs, available to order, into the 1920s. Designers from the 1860s like William Morris, Christopher Dresser and Owen Jones owed a great debt indeed to Pugin.

Clive Wainwright
Victoria & Albert Museum, London
1994

INTRODUCTION.

THE present work originated in the following circumstance :—on visiting the studio of Mons. Durlét, the architect of Antwerp cathedral and designer of the new stalls, I was exceedingly struck by the beauty of a capital cast in plaster, hanging amongst a variety of models, which appeared to be a fine work of the thirteenth century. On asking if he would allow me to have a squeeze from it, he readily consented, but at the same time informed me, to my great surprise, that the foliage of which it was composed had been gathered from his garden, and by him cast and adjusted in a geometrical form round a capital composed of pointed mouldings. This gave me an entirely new view of medieval carving ; and, pursuing the subject, I became fully convinced that the finest foliage work in the Gothic buildings were all close approximations to nature, and that their peculiar character was chiefly owing to the manner of their arrangement and disposition.* During the same journey I picked up a leaf of dried thistle from a foreign ship unloading at Havre, and I have never seen a more beautiful specimen of what we should

* See the doorway into the chapter-house at Southwell Minster, where the capitals, hollows, &c. are encircled with leaves of various plants, most naturally wrought. Many of the capitals of the lateral shafts in the Sainte Chapelle at Paris are composed of branches of rose trees, exquisitely worked from the natural plants. Instances of similar enrichments can be multiplied without number, from the first pointed down to the latest period.

usually term Gothic foliage : the extremities of the leaves turned over so as to produce the alternate interior and exterior fibres, exactly as they are worked in carved pannels of the fifteenth century, or depicted in illuminated borders. The more carefully I examined the productions of the medieval artists, in glass painting, decorative sculpture, or metal work, the more fully I was convinced of their close adherence to natural forms.

At the beginning of this work I have introduced a plate of glass remains, taken from antient examples in the Kentish churches; and also a variety of painted enrichments from various churches in Norfolk and Suffolk,* which will fully justify this assertion. It is absurd, therefore, to talk of *Gothic* foliage. The foliage is *natural*, and it is the *adaptation* and *disposition* of it which stamps the style. The great difference between antient and modern artists in their adaptation of nature for decorative purposes, is as follows. The former disposed the leaves and flowers of which their design was composed into geometrical forms and figures, carefully arranging the stems and component parts so as to *fill up* the space they were intended to enrich; and they were represented in such a manner as not to destroy the consistency of the peculiar feature or object they were employed to decorate, by merely imitative rotundity or shadow ; for instance, a pannel, which by its very construction is flat, would be ornamented by leaves or flowers drawn out or extended, so as to display their geometrical forms on a flat surface. While, on the other hand, a modern painter would

---

* A vast deal of wood-work, richly painted and gilt, is still remaining in the parish churches in these counties, principally on chancel screens. The most remarkable examples are at Ranworth, Trunch, Cawston, Worsted, and Southwold. The flowers and foliage are most gracefully depicted; the natural forms and outlines being accurately preserved. Many of the pannelled ceilings in these churches are decorated in a similar manner, with garlands of leaves and flowers branching out into the angles of the mouldings.

endeavour to give a fictitious idea of relief, as if *bunches* of flowers were laid on, and, by dint of shadow and foreshortening, an appearance of cavity or projection would be produced on a feature which architectural consistency would require to be treated as a plane; and instead of a well-defined, clear, and beautiful enrichment, in harmony with the construction of the part, an irregular and confused effect is produced, at utter variance with the main design.

The present work has been produced for the dissemination of these principles, and to assist in removing the reproach of mere servile imitation, so often cast on those who work after the antient manner. *Nature* supplied the medieval artists with all their forms and ideas; the same inexhaustible source is open to us: and if we go to the *fountain head*, we shall produce a multitude of beautiful designs treated in the same spirit as the old, but new in form. We have the advantage of many important botanical discoveries which were unknown to our ancestors; and surely it is in accordance with the true principles of art, to avail ourselves of all that is beautiful for the composition of our designs.

I trust, therefore, that this work may be the means of leading designers back to *first principles*; and that as by repeated copying the spirit of the original work is liable to be lost, so in decoration the constant reproduction of old patterns, without reference to the natural type for which they were composed, leads to debased forms and spiritless outline, and in the end to a mere caricature of a beautiful original. It is impossible to improve on the works of God; and the natural outlines of leaves, flowers, &c. must be more perfect and beautiful than any invention of man. As I have stated above, the great skill of the antient artists was in the *adaptation* and *disposition* of their forms. The present effort can only be considered as a mere sketch of what can be produced on those principles. As the patterns are principally intended for stencilling, those colours most in use have been selected; but in many cases the natural colour as well as form would greatly improve the effect. As regards the nomenclature of the plants, &c. selected, I have taken it from a very curious and beautiful old botanical work, entitled, " Tabernæ montanus eicones Plantarum," printed at Francfort in 1590. If there are any errors or singularities in any of the names engraved on the plates, they are taken from the work in question, as I am unfortunately not sufficiently learned in botany to distinguish any mistake in these respects.

A. WELBY PUGIN.

St. Augustine's, Ramsgate,
Feast of St. Michael, 1849.

LIST OF PLATES

LIST OF PLATES

2.

H C Maguire chromolith.   M. & N. Hanhart Chromolith. Imp.   † Pugin

3.

H.C. Maguire chromolith.   M. & N. Hanhart   Chromolith. Imp.   A Pugin

Glass Quarrels for Old Kentish Churches

4.

H.C. Maguire chromolith.   M. & N. Hanhart Chromolith. Imp.   Pugin

1, 2, 9 & 11. Ranworth church, Norfolk.   3 & 8. Dunstanton church, Norfolk.   4. Trunch church, Norfolk.

5, 6, 7 & 12 Southwold church.   10. Blighburgh church.

H C Maguire chromolith.   M. & N. Hanhart Chromolith. Imp.

1. Oxys floribus enteis   2. Cyperus dulcis Theophrasti   3. Absinthium marinum   4. Acarna Theophrasti Anguillaræ   5. Iva muschata

H.C Maguire chromolith.   M. & N. Hanhart   Chromolith. Imp.   ✠ Pugin

1. Caryophyllus montanus   2. Lychnis sylvestris purpurea   3. Camphorata Monspelica   4. Viola Martia purpurea   5. Lychnis arvensis

1. Pyromelo 2. Colocynthus mas 3. Finnaria latifolia major 4. Thlaspi Pannonicum 5. Primula veris

H.C Maguire chromolith   M. & N. Hanhart   Chromolith. Imp.   ✝ Pugin

1. Spartium Hispaniarum   2. Cytisus cornutus   3. Anemone major alba   4. Genista   5. Cytisus adulterinus

1. Cucumis Turcicus   2. Ornithogalum luteum   3. Absinthium album   4. Narcissus polyanthus Matthioli   5. Leucotum violaceum

1. Sonchus sylvaticus 2. Reseda latifolia 3. Anemones Chalcedonica major 4. Ruta tenuifolia 5. Scabiosa major

H.C Maguire chromohth.   M. & N. Hanhart   Chromolith. Imp.

1. Scabiosa major Hispanica   2. Filipendula montana   3. Artemisia Dioscoridis   4. Fragrum trifolium fragiferum   5. Eufrasia cœrulea

H.C Maguire chromolith.	M. & N. Hanhart	Chromolith. Imp.

1. Geranium Rupertianum   2. Caryophyllus Carthusianorum   3. Geranium arvense   4. Lychnis plumaria   5. Jacea alba

M. & N. Hanhart. Chromolith. Imp.

1. Viola Martia arborescens lutea   2. Viola Martia purpurea multiplex   3. Fumaria bulbosa

4. Viola petræ lutea multiplex   5. Ocymastrum rubrum

H.C Maguire chromolith.   M. &. N. Hanhart   Chromolith. Imp.   Pugin

1. Ranunculus sylvestris minor   2. Viola canina   3. Absinthium ponticum Galeni   4. Cardamine trifolia   5. Viola hyemalis

15.

H.C. Maguire chromolith.   M. & N. Hanhart Chromolith. Imp.   ✠ Pugin

1. Phalangium Narbonense   2. Hieracium minus Dioscorides   3. Thalictrum Herba Sophia latifolia

4. Chondrilla alba   5. Sonchus lenis angustifolia.

16.

H C Maguire chromolith.   M. & N. Hanhart   Chromolith. Imp.   ⊥ Pugin

1. Rosa Englenteria   2. Rosa muscata alba   3. Libanotis   4. Cistus Ledon myrtifolium   5. Herba Benedicta

H C Maguire chromolith.   M. &. N. Hanhart Chromolith. Imp.   Pugin

1. Sonchus asper 2. Ranunculus dulcis 3. Artemisia tenuifolia 4. Frumentum anyleum 5. Phalangium non ramosum

1. Auricula ursi   2. Origanum Heracleoticum 3. Aquifolium 4. Telephium purpureum 5. Heliotropium minus.

1. Chamæitea   2. Iva muschata   3. Brassica Anglica   4. Lichnis plumaria   5. Lychnis sylvestris

H C Maguire chromolith.   M. & N. Hanhart   Chromolith. Imp.

1. Calamintha amensis   2. Thlaspi minus clypeotum   3. Abrotanum humile   4. Vulnaria   5. Cramen aquaticum

21.

H C Maguire chromolith.   M. &. N. Hanhart   Chromolith. Imp.

1. Maiorana sive Amaricus major   2. Viola lunaris   3. Flos Aphricanus minor flore simplici

4. Nasturtium petræum   5. Tormentilla consolida rubra

H C Maguire chromolith.   M. &. N. Hanhart   Chromolith. Imp.   + Pugin

I. Ocymastrum rubrum   2. Lychnis sylvestris 3. Absinthium montanum seu Romanum 4. Vaccaria 5. Flos cuculi

H.C Maguire chromolith.   M. & N. Hanhart   Chromolith. Imp.

1. Cramen vulgare   2. Filipendula Saxifraga rubra   3. Buphtalmum   4. Lychnis plumaria   5. Herba articularis

H C Maguire chromolith   M. & N. Hanhart   Chromolith. Imp.   AWN Pugin

1. Lilium Saracenicum   2. Persoonia flexifolia   3. Fuchsia gracilis   4. Sytyrium triphyllon   5. Lilium album

6. Triorchis major mas   7. Ribes triflorum   8. Carduus lanceolatus   9. Bryngium Alpinum cœruleum

1 2 3 4 5

H C Maguire chromolith. M. & N. Hanhart Chromolith. Imp.

1. Fumaria bulbosa   2. Fumaria bulbosa   3. Fumaria bulbosa   4. Geranium violaceum   5. Curcubita largenaria major

26.

1. Dipsacus   2. Carduus lanceolatus   3. Melanthium agreste Nigella arvensis   4. Periclimenum   5. Tithymalus minimus

27.

1. Ilex coccifera   2. Fumaria latifolia minor   3. Quinquefolium Theophrasti   4. Hypericum Alexandrinum   5. Jasminium cœruleum

28

1

2

3

4

5

H C. Maguire chromolith.   M. & N. Hanhart   Chromolith. Imp.

1. Trifolium bituminosum   2. Trifolium cordatum   3. Cumerium sylvestre   4. Oxys floribus luteis   5. Fragum trifolium

29.

H C Maguire chromolith.   M. &. N. Hanhart Chromolith. Imp.

1. Alsine hedezacea   2. Plantago aquatica minor   3. Malva arborea   4. Tithymalus pazalius Matholi   5. Arcania Theophrasti

6. Chrysosplenon   7. Saxifrage alba

H. C. Maguire chromolith.   M. & N. Hanhart   Chromolith. Imp.   ✠ Pugin

1. Holostium umbellatum   2. Herba benedicta   3. Lysimachia minor   4. Convolvus cœruleus   5. Panaces costinum
6. Soldanella   7. Hypericum Alexandrinum   8. Volubilis major

31.

H.C Maguire chromolith.   M. & N. Hanhart   Chromolith. Imp.   ℉ Pugin

1. Lilium marinum album   2. Narcissus juncifolius   3. Narcissus medioluteus   4. Cytisus aduterinus   5. Pseudonarcissus luteus

6. Ledum Alpinum   7. Vitis idæa IV   8. Narcissus medioluteus   9. Cytysus I   10. Tithymalus amygdaloides

Fumaria bulbosa

Fumaria Bulbosa

Geranium violaceum

Cucurbita Lagenaria major

Fumaria Bulbosa

Pugin's preliminary watercolour for plate 25

FLORAL

ORNAMENT

DESIGNED by A·WELBY PUGIN.

Considerate lilia agri quomodo crescunt. amen dico vobis quoniam nec salomon in omnia gloria sua coopertus est sicut unum ex ipsis.

Pugin's trial watercolour for the title page of the 1849 edition of Floriated Ornament, now the front cover